P9-CJV-532

Earth's Core and Mantle

EARTH'S CORE AND MANTLE

HEAVY METAL, MOVING ROCK

GREGORY L. VOGT, Ed.D.

TWENTY-FIRST CENTURY BOOKS · MINNEAPOLIS

Text copyright © 2007 by Gregory L. Vogt

All rights reserved. International copyright secured. No part of this book may be reproduced, stored in a retrieval system, or transmitted in any form or by any means—electronic, mechanical, photocopying, recording, or otherwise—without the prior written permission of Lerner Publishing Group, except for the inclusion of brief quotations in an acknowledged review.

Twenty-First Century Books
A division of Lerner Publishing Group
241 First Avenue North
Minneapolis, Minnesota U.S.A.

Website address: www.lernerbooks.com

Library of Congress Cataloging-in-Publication Data

Vogt, Gregory.
    Earth's core and mantle : heavy metal, moving rock / by Gregory L. Vogt.
        v.   cm. — (Earth's spheres)
    Includes bibliographical references and index.
    Contents: A world of many spheres—Taking the Earth's pulse—
The Earth's core and the origin of the moon—Uncovering the mantle
and asthenosphere—Interacting with the surface and beyond—Mission
to the core.
    ISBN-13: 978-0-7613-2837-7 (lib. bdg. : alk. paper)
    ISBN-10: 0-7613-2837-8 (lib. bdg. : alk. paper)
    1. Earth—Core—Juvenile literature. 2. Earth—Mantle—Juvenile
literature. [1. Earth—Core. 2. Earth—Mantle.] I. Title. II. Series: Vogt,
Gregory. Earth's Spheres.
QE509.2.V64 2007
551.1'1—dc22   2003023969

Manufactured in the United States of America
1 2 3 4 5 6 – DP – 12 11 10 09 08 07

CONTENTS

A WORLD OF MANY SPHERES

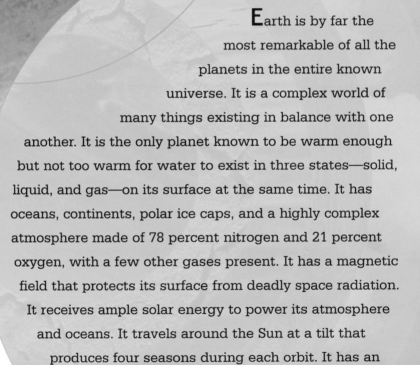

Earth is by far the most remarkable of all the planets in the entire known universe. It is a complex world of many things existing in balance with one another. It is the only planet known to be warm enough but not too warm for water to exist in three states—solid, liquid, and gas—on its surface at the same time. It has oceans, continents, polar ice caps, and a highly complex atmosphere made of 78 percent nitrogen and 21 percent oxygen, with a few other gases present. It has a magnetic field that protects its surface from deadly space radiation. It receives ample solar energy to power its atmosphere and oceans. It travels around the Sun at a tilt that produces four seasons during each orbit. It has an abundance of elements, including carbon, hydrogen, oxygen, and nitrogen, that enable living things to flourish on its surface. It is a world upon which humans are able to live—and to wonder how it all came about.

Earth is a planet of many spheres. Earth's many-layered structure can be compared to a hard-boiled egg with a yolk surrounded by the white and then by the shell. Deep inside is a heavy metallic sphere, called the core. Surrounding it is another sphere of heated rock, called the mantle. The upper layer of the mantle, called the asthenosphere, is made of semisolid rock that moves and deforms very slowly under pressure.

Above the asthenosphere and gliding very slowly across its surface is the rigid crust upon which we live. About three-quarters of the crust is covered with water. This is the hydrosphere. The zone where life exists is called the biosphere.

Between Earth's crust and hydrosphere is a thin layer of air, called the atmosphere. Finally, we come to the outermost reaches of the atmosphere, where astronauts and satellites orbit Earth and Earth interacts with outer space. Here Earth's magnetic field and very thin traces of gas collide with the solar wind.

How did Earth come to be? What are the different spheres or layers made of? How do the different spheres relate to one another? How are they changing? How do we know about them? This book, one of several, begins the story of the physical and biological Earth. It focuses on the inner Earth—its core and mantle.

HOW WAS EARTH FORMED?

The story of how Earth originated begins with the creation of our solar system approximately 5 billion years ago. In its earliest days, you wouldn't recognize it. The early solar system was merely a gigantic cloud of gas and dust, which astronomers call a nebula. This nebula contained all the atoms and molecules that would eventually become the Sun, nine planets, more than a hundred moons, and trillions of comets, asteroids, and meteors.

The solar system nebula was formed from the debris left over after the explosion of one or more ancient stars. The heat and pressure from these explosions, called supernovas, forged atoms of iron, carbon, silicon, oxygen, and other natural elements now included in the periodic table. The atoms were scattered about the nebula, which was many light-years in distance from one edge to the other.

Every atom and particle within the solar nebula tugged on every other atom and particle with a tiny force called gravity. Together, the force of gravity from all the atoms and particles slowed the cloud's expansion but did not stop it. Then, for reasons unknown to astronomers, the solar nebula began to contract. Perhaps a pressure wave from

The solar system nebula was approximately 50 light-years (300 trillion miles, or 470 trillion kilometers) across.

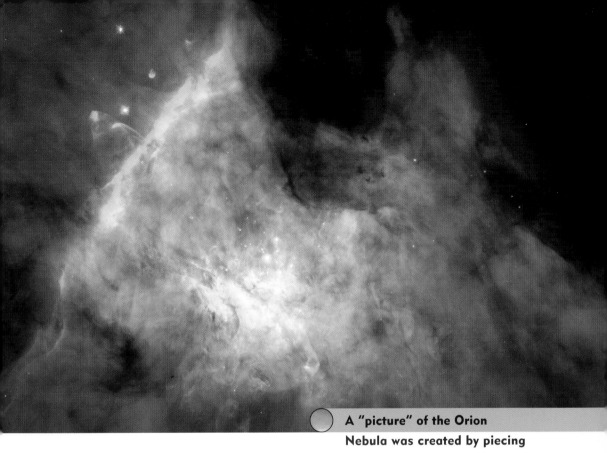

A "picture" of the Orion Nebula was created by piecing together a mosaic of forty-five images taken by the Hubble Space Telescope over a period of fourteen months. Though this view is about 2.5 light-years across, it is a small portion of the entire nebula. It does, however, include a star cluster and almost all the light from the bright, glowing clouds of gas that make up the nebula.

another exploding star started the atoms and particles moving back to the center of the nebula. Perhaps the contraction started with a strong gravitational wave caused by a passing star. Whatever the reason, the nebula began shrinking. As it did, the atoms and molecules in the nebula began passing very close to one another. Some got so close that their tiny gravitational attractions caused them to clump together. Their combined attractions caused nearby

HOW LONG AGO?

I t is difficult to imagine how long ago the solar system began. Scientists believe it began between 4.5 and 5 billion years ago. Since we humans live for only about 75 years, it is difficult to visualize 5 billion years. One way to do it is to shrink the entire life span of the solar system down to a 24-hour clock. Every second on the clock would equal about 58,000 years. At 0000 hours, or midnight, the solar system nebula begins to contract. At 0240, 2:40 A.M., Earth is created. The first simple life-forms begin appearing at 1200 hours, or noon. (The oldest fossils date to about 3.6 billion years.) Complex life-forms come into being at 2100 hours, or 9 P.M. The first human ancestors appear at about 2356:30, 3.5 minutes before 2400 hours, or midnight. If you live to be 100 years old, your entire life will pass in less than 0.002 second on this clock!

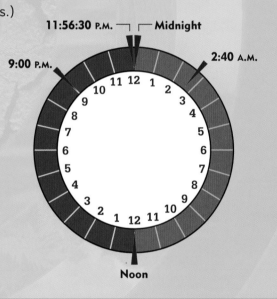

11:56:30 P.M. — ⌐ Midnight

9:00 P.M.

2:40 A.M.

Noon

atoms to join them. Ever so gradually, the tiny clumps grew. As they did, their gravitational attraction also grew, and they attracted more and more matter as the process continued. The clumps became dense swirls, like eddy currents in a flowing river.

Eventually, the clumps themselves joined together and the gravitational force continued to increase. While the clumps were forming, most of the atoms and dust particles started falling to the center of the solar nebula. The accumulation of matter there became much greater than anywhere else in the nebula. This was the start of the Sun. The Sun would not have been visible at first because the inward moving swarm of atoms and particles blocked the view. The Sun grew rapidly, and as it did, it began to get hot because of the large amount of matter slamming into it.

Because of the swirling, not all of the matter in the solar nebula fell to the center. Small amounts orbited the growing Sun. Imagine a lump of pizza dough. As the pizza cook twirls it in the air, it flattens out and becomes disk shaped. The same thing happened to the nebula as it swirled. The nebula flattened out into a broad disk. Astronomers call it an accretion disk.

Some of the physical principles that caused the nebula to flatten into a rotating disk around the Sun can be observed by watching someone swirl pizza dough. The motion causes the lump of dough to become wider and flatter with each swirl.

Small clumps of atoms and dust continued to grow in the accretion disk. These joined together and grew larger. Because there was comparatively little matter left in the disk, the clumps could become only so big. They became planets and moons. As they swung around the Sun, they swept up stray atoms and dust, thinning out the disk.

Perhaps a few hundred million years after the nebula began contracting (nobody knows for sure), the Sun ignited. Deep in the center of the Sun, atoms of hydrogen were squeezed together with pressures hundreds of billions of times greater than the pressure of air at Earth's surface. The temperature climbed to more than 18 million °F (10 million °C). A process

Deep inside the Sun, under tremendous pressure and extreme heat, atoms of hydrogen are fused to make atoms of helium. The process releases neutron particles and energy that travel through space to heat and light the solar system.

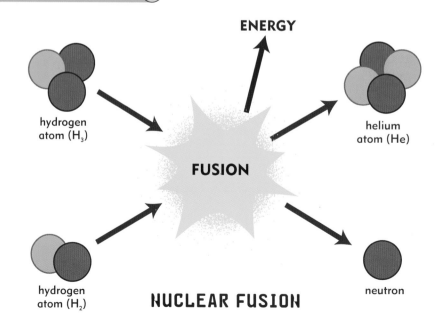

ENERGY

hydrogen atom (H$_3$)

helium atom (He)

FUSION

hydrogen atom (H$_2$)

neutron

NUCLEAR FUSION

This artwork shows Earthlike (rocky) planets forming in the early solar system. It is thought that the planets formed about 4.6 billion years ago from a rotating disk of material that formed at the same time as the Sun. The rocky inner planets formed by gathering up surrounding material, such as the rocky debris shown here, by gravitational attraction. Eventually four planets (Mars, Earth, Venus, and Mercury) survived, along with numerous asteroids. These small rocky planets contrast with the outer giant planets that consist mostly of gas and ice.

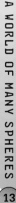

called nuclear fusion began. In the fusion reaction, two hydrogen atoms combine to form one helium atom. This was repeated trillions of times over. In each fusion reaction, small amounts of the hydrogen changed into heat and light energy that worked its way out from the Sun's center and poured into space. The energy flood blasted the remaining loose swarm of gas atoms and dust swirling around the Sun outward into space. Left behind were the planets and trillions of smaller objects—moons, asteroids, comets, and meteors.

By the time the Sun became a star, 99.8 percent of the

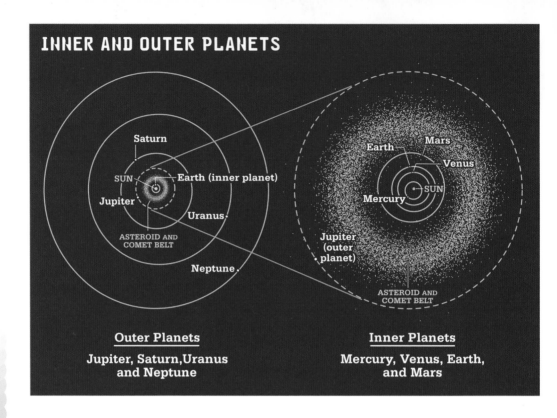

INNER AND OUTER PLANETS

Saturn

SUN — Earth (inner planet)

Jupiter

Uranus

ASTEROID AND
COMET BELT

Neptune

Earth   Mars

Venus

Mercury   SUN

Jupiter
(outer
planet)

ASTEROID AND
COMET BELT

Outer Planets
Jupiter, Saturn, Uranus
and Neptune

Inner Planets
Mercury, Venus, Earth,
and Mars

matter that existed in the solar nebula had fallen into the center. The planets and smaller bodies of the solar system came from the remaining 0.2 percent of the nebula.

The planets were of three kinds. Planets made mostly of rock and metal—Mercury, Venus, Earth, and Mars— circled the Sun in the inner solar system out to a distance of about 140 million miles (230,000 million km). Planets made mostly of liquid or frozen gas, the giant planets Jupiter, Saturn, Uranus, and Neptune, became the outer solar system, ranging from 480 million to 3 billion miles (780 million to 5 billion km) out. (Pluto, 4 billion miles (6 billion km) away, is a combination of ice and rock. Considered a planet since its discovery in 1930, Pluto was reassigned to a new category of heavenly body known as a "dwarf planet" in 2006.)

JUST THE FACTS

Earth is the largest of the inner planets in the solar system. It is about 7,950 miles (12,800 km) in diameter. Looking inward from its surface, we first see the lithosphere, or crust. It varies in thickness from 3 to 5 miles (5 to 8 km) for oceanic crust. Continental crust varies from a depth of 12 miles (20 km) to as much as 45 miles (70 km) under some of the higher mountain ranges. Just beneath the crust, we encounter the asthenosphere. This upper, somewhat elastic, layer of the mantle is about 300 miles (500 km) thick. It rests on the lower mantle, which is made of solid rock. The entire mantle is about 1,800 miles (2,900 km) thick. Beneath the mantle is a very hot molten rock layer, called the outer core. This layer is about 1,400 miles (2,200 km) thick. Finally, we reach the inner core, which is made up of iron and nickel metal. It is approximately 1,500 miles (2,400 km) in diameter.

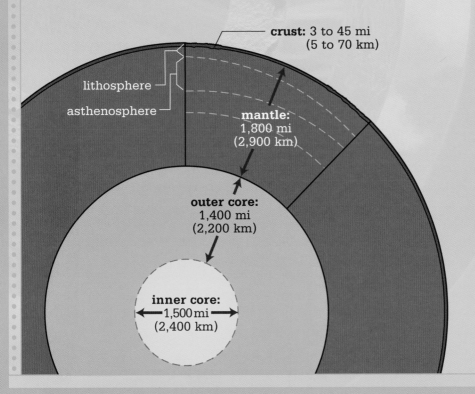

crust: 3 to 45 mi (5 to 70 km)

lithosphere

asthenosphere

mantle: 1,800 mi (2,900 km)

outer core: 1,400 mi (2,200 km)

inner core: 1,500 mi (2,400 km)

Scattered in orbits around all of the planets except Mercury and Venus are more than 160 moons. The larger of these moons, such as Earth's moon, are made of rock and metal. The smaller moons are made of rock, rock and ice, or ice.

In spite of the housecleaning by the Sun, the solar system, especially the inner system, was messy. Asteroids, comets, and meteors were raining upon Earth and the inner planets. The early Earth was completely molten and remained so for perhaps half a billion years. Gradually, the outer rock cooled to form a fragile crust that cracked and broke and melted again as it was continually slammed by asteroids and comets.

In time, most of the solar system debris fell to one planet or another. Earth's crust began to stabilize and grow thicker and harder as it cooled. The heavier molten materials, such as the elements iron and nickel, settled in its center. Lighter elements such as aluminum and silicon floated to the upper levels. With the formation of a relatively stable rocky crust, water began collecting on Earth's surface, and an atmosphere began to surround it. Most of the water collected in deep basins to become oceans. Small pieces of continents, called microcontinents, appeared; these pieces later combined to make larger continents. The oceans were like a chemical soup, and out of them came simple, early life-forms that grew and became more complex over time. Earth was on the way to becoming what it is today.

THE WINNER IS ZIRCON!

Geologists the world over hunt for rocks and minerals that formed when Earth was young. Like pictures in a photo album, ancient Earth materials provide clues about what the conditions were like when they formed. New discoveries are continually being made. Currently, the oldest-known rocks are volcanic and are found in northern Quebec. They are dated at about 3.8 billion years old. Other really ancient rocks are found in Minnesota, Greenland, and South Africa. The oldest material is not a rock but rather grains of the mineral zircon.

Age dating of one of the grains puts it at about 4.3 to 4.4 billion years. Zircon is a tough mineral, and the rock the grain was once a part of has long since been worn away. The ancient zircon grain got incorporated into newer rock. The results of these tests are causing geologists to rethink their ideas of when Earth's solid crust began forming.

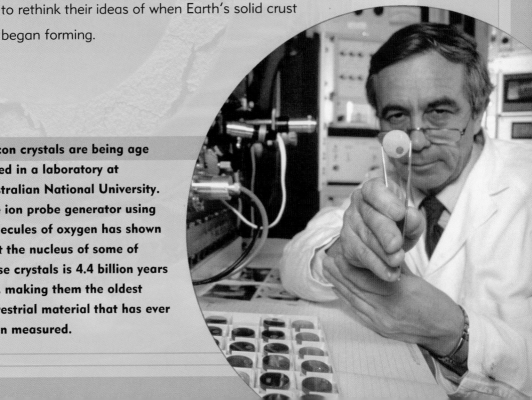

Zircon crystals are being age dated in a laboratory at Australian National University. The ion probe generator using molecules of oxygen has shown that the nucleus of some of these crystals is 4.4 billion years old, making them the oldest terrestrial material that has ever been measured.

CHAPTER 1

TAKING EARTH'S PULSE

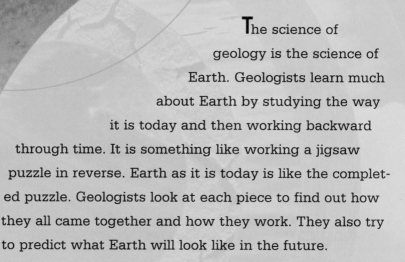

The science of geology is the science of Earth. Geologists learn much about Earth by studying the way it is today and then working backward through time. It is something like working a jigsaw puzzle in reverse. Earth as it is today is like the completed puzzle. Geologists look at each piece to find out how they all came together and how they work. They also try to predict what Earth will look like in the future.

One of the most difficult Earth puzzle pieces is Earth's interior because it is completely hidden from our view. However, we do know a great deal about what the insides of Earth look like and how they function. But that information didn't come from traveling there.

Science fiction stories and movies notwithstanding, no one has ever been to the core of Earth. There has never been a sample collected from the core by drilling. The deepest wells, mines, and caves on Earth are only pinpricks when compared to the size of Earth. Instead, what we know about Earth's interior is based primarily on a variety of scientific studies and experiments conducted from Earth's surface.

JUST HOW BIG?

Earth's inner and outer core make up a sphere nearly 4,300 miles (6,800 km) in diameter. The solid inner core by itself is about 1,500 miles (2,400 km) in diameter. That's about 600 miles (1,000 km) smaller than Earth's moon. The inner core and outer core together make up a sphere about the same size as the planet Mars!

diameter of Earth's inner core

diameter of Earth's moon

diameter of Earth's inner and outer cores

diameter of Earth's inner and outer cores

diameter of Mars

The solid earth, or crust, beneath our feet is anything but solid. It is cracked and broken in many places. The crust continually changes, with volcanoes erupting to pile new rock on the surface. Pressures several miles below the surface of the crust can periodically snap the rock, causing great earthquakes and gradually thrusting up large blocks of land to form mountains. Similar pressures can also cause rock to bend slowly, forming folded rocks. Such rocks can distort Earth's surface and form mountain ranges of alternating peaks and valleys, like blankets bunched up on a bed.

If you live on the East Coast of the United States, you experience very little earthquake and no volcano activity, but if you live on the West Coast, earthquakes and volcanoes are a part of life. As you can see on the map on the opposite page, Earth's crust is broken into giant continent-size plates that move slowly across the upper mantle. The North American plate, the crustal plate upon which most of the United States is located, is moving slowly westward, squeezing the Pacific Plate, which lies beneath the Pacific Ocean. On the Asian side, the plates are also pushing into the Pacific from the other direction. Great pressures build up in the crust where these plates collide, creating not only earthquakes but also a broad ring of mountains peppered with volcanoes that surround the Pacific Ocean basin. These mountains, shown as the orange area on the map, form what is known as the Ring of Fire.

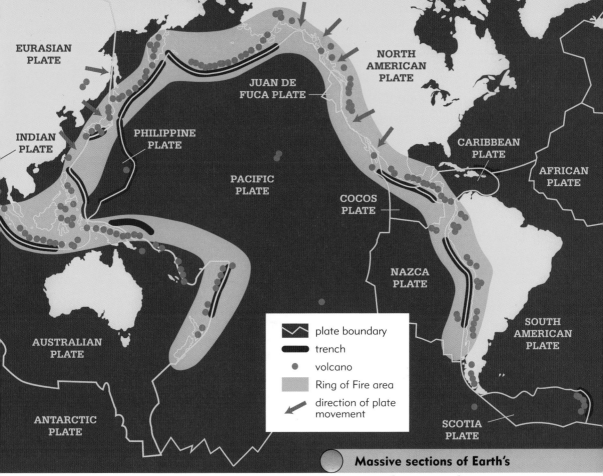

EURASIAN PLATE

JUAN DE FUCA PLATE

NORTH AMERICAN PLATE

INDIAN PLATE

PHILIPPINE PLATE

CARIBBEAN PLATE

AFRICAN PLATE

PACIFIC PLATE

COCOS PLATE

NAZCA PLATE

SOUTH AMERICAN PLATE

AUSTRALIAN PLATE

ANTARCTIC PLATE

SCOTIA PLATE

plate boundary
trench
volcano
Ring of Fire area
direction of plate movement

Massive sections of Earth's crust, known as plates, are constantly in motion, creating huge pressures as they collide.

ANCIENT CHINESE SECRET

China is one of the oldest learned societies. Long ago, Chinese scholars concerned themselves with earthquakes, because China experienced so many of them. The first scientific instrument to measure the occurrence of earthquakes was invented in China. The device, called a seismoscope, was built by Chang Heng in the year A.D. 132. It was a metal vessel that had eight dragon heads mounted around the top. Inside each dragon's mouth was a ball. Beneath the dragon heads were

The original seismoscope made by Chang Heng has not survived. This model was made from descriptions of the original instrument.

frogs with open mouths. It is not known what was inside the vessel, but scholars believe that there was some sort of pendulum that would swing when an earthquake was felt. One or more balls would be dislodged by the pendulum and fall into the frogs' mouths. It is not known if the device worked well.

Over the years, many different devices have been constructed for measuring earthquakes. The earliest ones just indicated that an earthquake had occurred. Later devices, called seismographs, recorded the time, duration, and even the strength of the quakes. It is with these seismographs that geologists have been able to piece together a picture of Earth's interior without seeing it directly.

Modern seismographs can measure earthquakes from great distances as information is transmitted through Earth's surface to sensors. Here a seismograph in Golden, Colorado, is displaying a massive earthquake (7.5 on the Richter scale) that is striking the coast of Mexico.

BLIND AS A BAT

Bats aren't really blind, but they do fly safely in some very dark places. They have sharp hearing and emit high-pitched squeaks that bounce off objects in their way. This process, known as echolocation, enables bats to determine how big and how far away objects are and how to fly around them.

Geologists use a similar process to study Earth's interior. They do it by listening to the vibrations, or seismic waves, caused by earthquakes around the world. To understand how this works, we first need to understand a few things about waves. When you toss a pebble into a

23

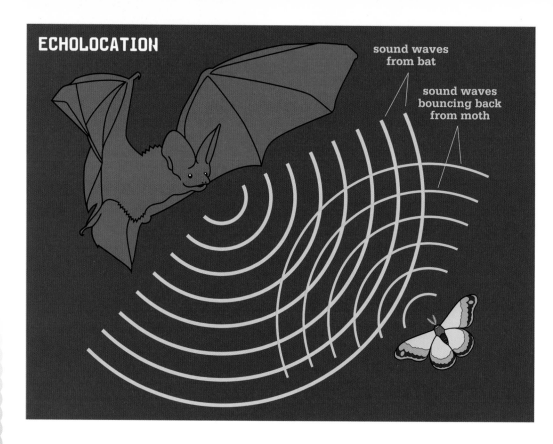

ECHOLOCATION

sound waves from bat

sound waves bouncing back from moth

pond of water, it creates a series of circular waves that expand outward. While it may look as if the water is flowing away from the point where the pebble entered, it is not. It is the energy of the falling pebble that is moving away. You can prove this by placing a cork or a twig in the water before you throw in the pebble. The cork or twig remains in the same place after the wave passes by.

Someone standing on the opposite side of the pond will know you tossed the pebble into the pond when the water ripples arrive, even if that person didn't actually see you toss the pebble. A second way that the person might know you tossed in a pebble is by hearing the splash. The sound travels through the air to that person's ears, but he or she doesn't have to be standing on the edge of the pond to hear it. The sound also travels through the water. Next time you are swimming in a pool, duck your head underwater just before someone jumps in. You will hear the splash through the water.

Sound is created by vibration. The vibrations in the air or the water carry the sound to your ears. As a matter of fact, the denser the material through which the vibrations are traveling, the easier and faster the vibrations travel. Try this experiment sometime. Find a long metal railing, and place your ear on it. Have a friend some distance away tap the railing. You will hear the tapping clearly through the railing, even though the sound traveling through the air may be faint. Furthermore, the sound through the railing will travel faster so that you will hear a second tap when the sound in the air catches up.

When an earthquake occurs, the energy released by the quake travels as seismic waves around and through Earth. It is these waves that are measured by seismographs. Three different waves are produced, and each has its own properties that make them useful to scientists.

Ships use a kind of echolocation, called SONAR (SOund Navigation And Ranging), for locating other ships, especially submarines, mapping ocean bottoms, and even locating fish. SONAR devices emit sounds underwater that bounce back from objects telling distance and direction, size, shape, and even speed.

Two of the waves travel through Earth, and the third runs across the surface.

When an earthquake occurs, the first wave to arrive at the seismograph is called the primary wave, or P-wave. A P-wave is very easy to visualize if you have a Slinky toy. With the help of a friend, stretch the Slinky out horizontally on a smooth hard surface, such as a desk or floor. Have your friend gather a couple of the Slinky's coils, stretch them back, and then release them. The motion that travels from your friend to you is a P-wave. You will

P-WAVE

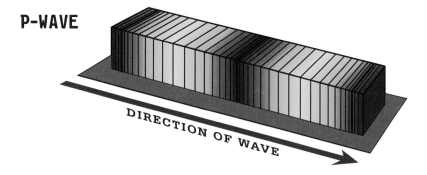

DIRECTION OF WAVE

see that the coils push together and then pull apart all along the Slinky in the same direction—and in the opposite direction from the direction in which the wave is traveling. P-waves travel through the earth.

The second kind of wave is known as an S-wave. It also travels through the earth, but travels more slowly than the P-wave. To see an S-wave, have a friend hold one end of a Slinky and you hold the other, stretching it out horizontally. Shake one end of the Slinky back and forth. You will see that the motion is at a right angle to the direction the wave

S-WAVE

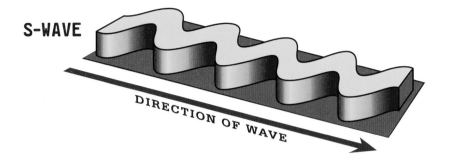

DIRECTION OF WAVE

is traveling. S-waves can travel easily through solid rock but are blocked by water or molten rock.

The slowest wave is the L-wave. It runs across Earth's surface. It is the kind of surface wave that is made when you toss a pebble in a pond. You can also make the L-wave by shaking one end of the Slinky up and down.

L-WAVE

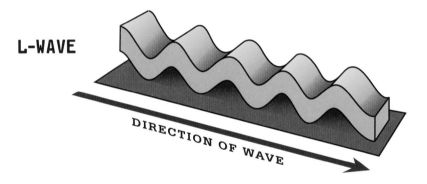

DIRECTION OF WAVE

Seismographs around the world detect about 500,000 earthquakes every year. About one in five is large enough for people to feel, and about 100 cause significant damage to Earth's surface. The amount of damage done, in part, depends upon how strong an earthquake is and how close it is to a city. Over short distances, P-waves and S-waves arrive almost simultaneously. The shaking caused by the two, one after another, can be intense. Buildings and other structures are literally shaken to pieces. How

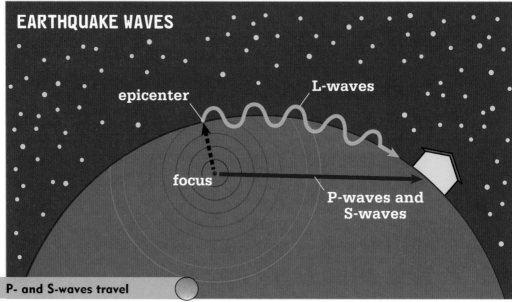

EARTHQUAKE WAVES

epicenter

L-waves

focus

P-waves and
S-waves

**P- and S-waves travel
through the solid Earth.
L-waves travel on the
surface, starting at the point
immediately above the focus.**

did the different kinds of waves enable scientists to find Earth's core? When an earthquake shatters and moves huge blocks of rock deep in the crust, P-waves and S-waves are driven through Earth while L-waves race across its surface. Seismographs around the world will register these waves as they arrive. Depending upon where a seismograph is located, something interesting happens. If it is on the exact opposite side of Earth from the quake, it will feel the P-waves some minutes after the quake occurred. Later, it will record the L-waves—but the S-waves will not arrive. Scientists quickly figured out that something was blocking the S-waves. Remember, S-waves do not travel through liquid. They hypothesized that there must be liquid, in the form of molten rock, deep within Earth. By comparing the data from many seismographs spaced around the world, scientists discovered that S-waves are felt only when the seismograph is no farther than one-quarter of the way around Earth from the quake. Any farther away and the S-waves are blocked!

With careful mapping of Earth's insides, it was determined that the S-waves are being blocked by a large mass of molten material 1,800 miles (2,900 km) beneath the surface—Earth's core. Further wave studies told them that the molten material did not go all the way to Earth's center. At 3,170 miles (5,100 km) below the surface, the material becomes solid again and remains that way all the way to the center. They figured this out by mapping the way P-waves bend and change direction when they pass through materials of different density. It is something like the way a drinking straw appears to bend when it is in a glass of water. Studies of earthquake waves helped geologists discover that Earth has a solid inner core surrounded by a molten outer core.

Seismographs have also been used on the Moon to learn about its interior. Apollo astronauts set up seismographs to measure moonquake vibrations. They detected a small core about 400 miles (640 km) in diameter.

CRUSHING WATER

Every now and then, we are reminded of the awesome power of Earth. Small readjustments of Earth's crust can have unimaginable consequences for living things on the surface. On December 26, 2004, at seven in the morning, local time, a 600-mile (970 km) stretch of ocean floor off the west coast of Indonesia suddenly shifted in a massive earthquake. It was the fifth-worst earthquake to hit Earth since 1900. The shift took place where the segment of the crust called the Indian Plate slides under the Burmese Plate. The movement was small when compared to the thickness of the crust, perhaps 60 feet (20 m), but it released huge amounts of energy. Billons of tons of ocean water were set into motion. The water surged outward in all directions at the speed of a jet airliner.

Across the open ocean, the widely spaced waves were only a few feet high and hardly noticeable. That all changed when they arrived at the shorelines of Indonesia, Thailand, India, and Africa. Friction with the shallow bottoms slowed the waves and caused them to mound up as much as 60 feet (20 m). The waves are known as tsunamis. It is a Japanese term and means "seismic sea wave."

It was still morning when the tsunamis arrived at the shoreline around the Indian Ocean. Unsuspecting bathers on the beaches saw walls of racing water. When they realized the danger and began running inland, it was too late. The waves pounded coastal communities, scraping away homes, uprooting trees, flinging fishing boats, tumbling automobiles and trucks, and smashing bridges. The water smashed onto the land and then roared back into the ocean in a powerful one-two punch.

The numbers of casualties kept climbing as reports from hard-hit areas slowly trickled in. The exact number will never be known because many

This photo, taken near Phuket, Thailand, shows the powerful wall of water created by the December 26, 2004, tsunami. The wave is just starting its devastating sweep inland, where it will destroy virtually everything in its path.

bodies were buried in mud or washed out to sea. By the end of 2005, the number stood at more than 216,000 people dead and missing in eleven countries. The number of casualties continued to climb after the tsunami as survivors suffered from diseases that began spreading in the aftermath.

Tsunamis are a fact of life for coastal communities in earthquake-prone regions. A tsunami-warning network of instruments is operating in the Pacific Ocean where the seismic sea waves are common. Even a few minutes of warning could save thousands of lives. No such network is at work in the Indian Ocean. The last significant tsunami there occurred more than 120 years ago when the volcanic island of Krakatoa exploded. Forty thousand people were killed directly by the explosion or indirectly by the tsunamis kicked up by it. Hopefully, a warning network for the Indian Ocean will be established in time for the next earthquake, which will surely come.

CHAPTER 2

EARTH'S CORE AND THE ORIGIN OF THE MOON

Where did Earth's moon come from? Many planets in the solar system have moons, and Earth's moon is an especially big one. We can see the Moon's surface clearly with telescopes. In the twentieth century, rockets, computers, and robots were combined to send the first probes to the lunar surface. Astronauts then followed the probes to the Moon's surface. From 1969 to 1972, six spindly Apollo manned spacecraft gently touched down on the surface of the Moon. Pairs of space-suited astronauts climbed down ladders and began exploring the surface. They set up scientific experiments, took many pictures, and collected samples of rock and sediment. It took three days to get to the Moon, but the astronauts

In their December 1972 mission to the Moon, *Apollo 17* astronauts Eugene Cernan and Harrison Schmitt collected samples in the Taurus-Littrow valley. They returned to Earth with 240 pounds (110 kg) of rock and soil samples, more than from any other lunar landing sites.

were only able to spend a few hours working on its surface. They worked quickly because the real study of the Moon would take place back on Earth. Thousands of scientists eagerly awaited the astronauts' return with their precious cargo of pieces of the Moon. By the end of the Apollo program, more than 840 pounds (380 kilograms) of lunar rock and sediment were brought back from the Moon.

Prior to the Apollo missions, scientists had a number of hypotheses about where the Moon came from. One was that the Moon was merely a small, or minor, planet

This lunar sample brought back to Earth by the *Apollo 15* astronauts is a volcanic igneous rock—formed from solidified lava.

that passed too near Earth and was captured into orbit by the combined gravitational pulls of the two bodies on each other. In another hypothesis, the Moon was formed as a companion at the same time as Earth from the debris in the nebula. In still another hypothesis, the Moon was once a piece of Earth. Perhaps Earth was spinning so rapidly in its early days that part of it split off and was flung into space. To support this hypothesis, some scientists had observed that the volume of the Moon was roughly equal to the volume of the Pacific Ocean basin.

Scientists hoped that the Moon rocks and sediment brought back to Earth by the astronauts would provide them with the information to determine which theory was correct. What they discovered told them not only about the Moon's origin but also about the origin of Earth's core. Today most scientists think the Moon was created in a terrible explosion that occurred when a Mars-sized planet collided with Earth. At the time, the two planets were still young and mostly molten. Most of the heavier material in the smaller planet, such as iron and nickel, sank to Earth's center, combining with the metal already present there. (Compared to the present-day Earth, the Moon has little iron in it. It would have relatively similar amounts if any of the other hypotheses were true.) At the same time, a great splash of debris and vapor, leftovers from the collision, spun out into a disk-shaped orbit around Earth. Gradually the debris in the disk became absorbed into the smaller mass, which formed the Moon.

MORE PROOF FOR THE CORE

Seismographic observation isn't the only data pointing to the presence of a two-layered core inside Earth. Earth's gravitational attraction also provides important data.

By studying the pull of Earth's gravity on other objects, scientists can estimate what Earth's mass is. The mass is a measure of the amount of matter in something. In the case of Earth, the mass is a huge number. Earth's mass in pounds is the number 1,316 followed by 22 zeros (in kilograms, 597 followed by 22 zeros). That's about 6,500 million million million tons. It is also possible to determine Earth's volume, and this leads to knowing what its density is.

SHE DISCOVERED EARTH'S INNER CORE

About fifty years after the invention of the seismograph, Danish seismologist Inge Lehmann *(below)* analyzed waves from an earthquake that occurred near New Zealand in 1929. Some of the waves she studied should have been deflected by Earth's core, but they acted, instead, as though they had bounced off some kind of barrier. Working in the days before computers, Lehmann organized data about many earthquakes on cards that she sorted in cardboard oatmeal boxes. By 1936 she published a paper entitled "P-Prime" in which she proposed a new model of Earth's core. Her paper suggested that Earth's core has a discontinuity, or change, in its composition that divides it into an outer and inner core. The discontinuity Lehmann discovered is known as the Lehmann discontinuity. It wasn't until 1970, when much more accurate seismographs than Lehmann used were developed, that her hypothesis was proved. Lehmann was born in Denmark in 1888. She helped set up the first seismic networks in Denmark and Greenland and soon became the first chief of seismology at the Royal Danish Geodetic Institute. Inge Lehmann died in 1993 at the age of 105.

Density is a measure of how much matter is packed into something compared to an equal volume of water. Earth's density is 5.5, or 5.5 times heavier than a body of the same size made up entirely of liquid water.

This was an important finding because the rocks on Earth's surface have an average density of 3. That means the inside of Earth must be denser than the outside in order for the whole planet to have an average density of 5.5. The scientists did some calculating. In order to average 5.5, the rock near Earth's center would have to have a density of about 15. No known rock has that density. Furthermore, the pressure of all the rock weighing down on Earth's center would not be sufficient to squeeze the rock to a density of 15. Something else was happening.

Meteorites that fell to Earth from space gave scientists some important clues that Earth might have a large core of very dense material. Earth is believed to be about four and a half billion years old. Age dating of meteorites shows that they are the same age. In other words, Earth and meteorites formed from the solar system nebula at

Most of the Moon rocks collected by the Apollo astronauts are 3 to 4 billion years old. Few rocks on Earth are that age. The Moon doesn't have water and wind erosion like that which has wiped away most of Earth's ancient surface rocks.

Scientists collect meteorites for study because they are believed to be unchanged fragments of the material from which the planets and the Moon were made. There are two main types of meteorites. Stony meteorites *(left)* are made of stony minerals mixed with particles of iron. Iron meteorites *(right)* consist mainly of iron combined with nickel.

the same time out of the same materials.

Meteorites come in many forms. Some are made of rock, some are made of metal, and some are made of metal and rock mixed together. Scientists have carefully analyzed the metal meteorites and found that they are made mostly of iron, with about 8 percent nickel, some cobalt, and smaller amounts of sulfur, silica, and carbon. The density of these meteorites is about 8. If Earth had a core made from the same material as metal meteorites, scientists could explain the 5.5 average density of the planet. Since they knew the size of the core from seismographic data, they could calculate its mass if it were made of the same stuff as metal meteorites. Although the core is only about 10 percent of the total volume of Earth, it accounts for about 30 percent of Earth's mass. They concluded that the 4,300-mile-diameter (6,800 km) core made mostly of molten and solid iron and nickel would average out Earth's density at 5.5.

LIQUID AND SOLID

One of the interesting questions about Earth's core has to do with the states of the material that make up the inner and outer layers. The common states of matter are solids, liquids, and gases. Earth's inner core is solid, but the outer core is liquid. Why? You would think it would be the other way around.

The core is extremely hot. At its very center, it is about 9,000°F (5,000°C), or hotter than the surface of the Sun. It is easily hot enough to melt the iron and nickel that make up the inner core. Instead, these metals are solid. However, the outer core, where temperatures are cooler, is molten.

The explanation for the reversal of states has to do with pressure. If it weren't for pressure, both the inner and outer core would be molten due to the high temperatures. In fact, there would not be an inner and outer core because there wouldn't be any boundaries. It would all just be molten.

PACKING OF ATOMS IN SOLIDS, LIQUIDS, AND GASES

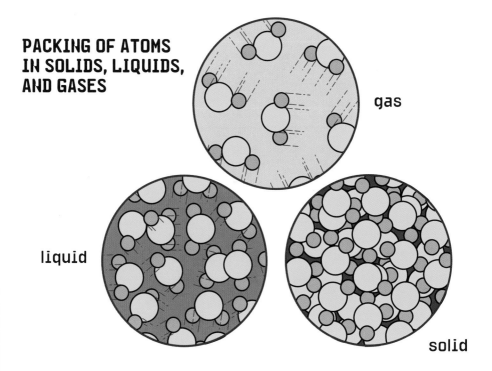

gas

liquid

solid

Like all elements, the iron and nickel in the core are made up of atoms. How closely the atoms are packed together determines the state. A gas is made up of widely spaced atoms that travel great distances before bumping into other atoms. In liquids, the atoms are packed very closely together, but they still can move around. In solids, the atoms are jammed together so that they can vibrate but cannot change positions. To understand this idea, think of an elevator car with just two people. The two people can move about but occasionally bump into each other. Put another four people in the elevator, and the people can still move, but they have to move around one another and bump more often. Jam the elevator to capacity, and everybody is stuck where they are standing. They can wiggle, but they can't move.

Earth's outer core is like the elevator car with six people. It is hot enough in the outer core to melt metal, but it is not so squeezed (packed together) by the weight of the mantle and crust above to prevent the atoms from moving around. The inner core is like the elevator car jammed with people. The atoms are under so much pressure that they can't move about even in the high temperatures. The iron and nickel atoms are packed so tightly that they actually form crystals. The crystals look like those that are exposed when iron/nickel meteorites are sliced open.

How much pressure is there in the inner core? When you stand at the shore of an ocean, the air pressure weighing down on every square inch of your skin is about 14.7 pounds (6.67 kg). If you were standing in the center of the inner core, the pressure would be more than 3 million times greater!

The pressure at the center of Earth is estimated to be 3.6 million times the air pressure at sea level on Earth's surface.

CHAPTER 3

UNCOVERING the MANTLE AND ASTHENOSPHERE

Lying on top of Earth's core is the mantle. Similar to the solid/liquid core beneath, the mantle is also layered, although geologists are less certain of the actual size of the layers. The lower part of the mantle, resting on the liquid outer core, is made of solid rock. Above that is a middle layer consisting of semisolid rock. Finally comes a layer called the asthenosphere. Things get a little confusing here because the asthenosphere is not a distinct layer. Its upper zone blends into Earth's crust. Asthenosphere rock is elastic—that is, it can slowly stretch and flow. Crustal rock lies on top of the asthenosphere. Because the asthenosphere rock is elastic, the crust is able to slowly glide across its surface.

DISCOVERING THE MANTLE

Previously, we saw that earthquakes create waves that travel across Earth's surface and through the interior. We found out that body waves bend as they encounter new materials. Because of the bending, scientists could measure the extent of Earth's core. The bending also enabled scientists to measure and model the mantle.

The first indications that Earth had a mantle came to light with an earthquake in the Kupa valley, in Croatia, in 1909. Andrija Mohorovičić, a seismologist in Yugoslavia, studied this quake and others and noticed that some of the body waves measured with the seismograph arrived more quickly than expected. He eventually concluded that these body waves had passed from Earth's crust into some new material. The speed of the waves had increased in the new material. Mohorovičić discovered the bottom of Earth's crust. The boundary was later verified by other scientists and in honor of Mohorovičić, they called the boundary the Mohorovičić discontinuity. Since the name is difficult to say, it was quickly replaced by the nickname Moho.

The elevation of the Moho varies across Earth. This is because of buoyancy. If you fill a glass bowl with water and then cover it with a layer of ice cubes, you will see buoyancy at work. The ice cubes float, but most of the ice is below the water's surface. If you heap more ice cubes in the center of the bowl, you will start forming a mountain. The top of the pile of ice will be above the water

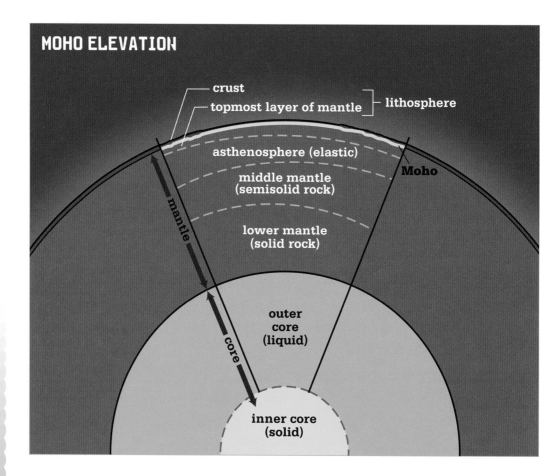

MOHO ELEVATION

crust

topmost layer of mantle ⎤ lithosphere

asthenosphere (elastic)

Moho

middle mantle
(semisolid rock)

mantle

lower mantle
(solid rock)

outer
core
(liquid)

core

inner core
(solid)

while the lower ice cubes are pushed deeper into the water. The ice is like Earth's crust. Thin crust does not press much into the asthenosphere, while thick crust presses deeply into the asthenosphere.

Since we live on Earth's outside, we know much about the shape of the crust. The thin places in the crust lie chiefly beneath ocean basins. The crust there averages just over 3 miles (5 km). The crust under the continents is much thicker. Estimates vary, but continental crust averages about 20 miles (30 km), but can be as much as 45 miles (70 km) thick under tall mountain ranges.

WHAT IS THE MANTLE MADE OF?

The composition of Earth's mantle is easier to guess at than the composition of the core. Although most of the mantle is well beyond the reach of geologists, some of the material in the mantle occasionally reaches Earth's surface. Sometimes this happens during volcanic eruptions. Volcanoes are created when molten rock works its way from deep inside Earth to the surface. It either pours out as a river of lava, or it explodes out because of a high content of gas mixed in (something like the way a soft drink will sometimes explode when the cap is removed).

The mantle experiences great heat and pressure.

WHERE DOES THE HEAT COME FROM?

Earth's interior heat comes from two sources. One source is the heat generated as the solar system formed. Matter piling upon matter to build Earth out of the great nebula caused tremendous amounts of heat to be generated and stored inside. The other source of heat is the radioactive decay of elements such as uranium, potassium, and thorium. As these elements in the mantle and crust break down into other elements, they release tiny amounts of heat that accumulate. About half of Earth's present-day heat is left over from Earth's formation. The rest comes from radioactive decay.

EARTH IS COOLING OFF

Miners descending into deep mine passages will tell you that the temperature of rock increases with depth. The temperature change is about 45°F per mile (25°C/km) beneath the surface. Like a freshly baked loaf of bread set out on a rack to cool, the outside of the bread cools first. Soon it is possible to pick up the loaf with bare hands while the inside is still too hot to touch. Earth's outside is cool because much of the surface heat has been transferred to the atmosphere, where it can escape to space. The internal heat is slowly escaping as volcanoes erupt and spew hot lava on the surface. The flowing lava carries heat from below and releases it into the atmosphere. Hot springs, vents, and geysers also release internal heat into the atmosphere.

Geysers and volcanoes act similarly. While volcanoes spew out melted rock, geysers send out water containing dissolved minerals.

Parts of Earth consist of piled-up sheets of lava. The Hawaiian Islands, the location of the lava flow shown here, are built mainly of lava. The Columbia lava plateau in the northeastern United States is made up of a pile of lava almost 1 mile (1.6 km) thick in places.

When the conditions are right, molten material begins to melt and force its way to the surface. The lava that cools from the molten material will have elements that were once part of the mantle. Some lava may even have tiny crystals that formed deep beneath the surface.

Another way mantle material makes its way to the surface is through mountain building and erosion. Many mountains are created when the crust is pressed from the sides. Over millions of years, the bending and breaking of this rock thrusts up rock hundreds of miles above sea

Perovskites are a large family of crystalline ceramics that derive their name from a specific mineral known as perovskite. The mineral perovskite was first described in the 1830s by the geologist Gustav Rose, who named it after the famous Russian mineralogist Count Lev Aleksevich von Perovski.

level. Much later, the forces of erosion wear away these mountains, exposing their roots (for example, the Appalachian Mountains). Sometimes rock thought to have formed in the uppermost part of the mantle may be found in these roots.

From exposed mantle rock and the information gained by seismographs, scientists believe the mantle is mostly made of rocky material rather than metal. The rock has some iron, titanium, and

magnesium, but it has large quantities of elements such as oxygen, silicon, aluminum, calcium, and potassium— this list is in order of abundance. The elements are assembled into tightly packed mineral crystals such as the transparent green olivine, the reddish garnet, and the metallic gray perovskite. Perovskite, made of the elements calcium, titanium, and oxygen, is thought to be the most common mineral found in the lower mantle. Considering that the mantle makes up almost 70 percent of Earth's total mass, perovskite may be Earth's most common mineral as well.

CHAPTER 4

INTERACTING WITH THE SURFACE AND BEYOND

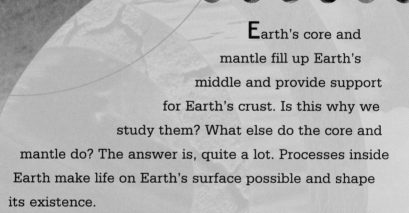

Earth's core and mantle fill up Earth's middle and provide support for Earth's crust. Is this why we study them? What else do the core and mantle do? The answer is, quite a lot. Processes inside Earth make life on Earth's surface possible and shape its existence.

EARTH HAS A LOT OF PULL

With or without a core, Earth would still have a gravitational field. All objects, no matter how small, have gravity. However, for a planet to have a substantial gravitational field, one strong enough to hold an atmosphere, a great deal of matter has to be concentrated in one place. Neither Earth's moon nor the planet Mercury has enough matter to hold an atmosphere. The Moon's gravity is only one-sixth that of Earth. Gas molecules in an atmosphere are in constant motion. They travel at great speeds for short distances before they bump into one another. The bumping produces atmospheric pressure. A lot of bumping goes on in Earth's atmosphere, and this produces a pressure of 14.7 pounds per square inch (101 kilopascals) at sea level. In spite of the pressure on Earth, the atmosphere stays together because gravity holds it down. A molecule of gas on Earth has to travel faster than 7 miles (11 km) per second to escape Earth's gravity. On the Moon, gas molecules have to go only about 1.5 miles (2.4 km) per second to escape. This is a speed the molecules can easily reach. Furthermore, on the sunlit side of the Moon, the temperature is hotter than on Earth, and gas molecules move faster as the heat increases.

The planet Mercury doesn't have an atmosphere, even though it is larger than the Moon. Its gravity is 0.38 the gravity of Earth. Normally, this would be enough to hold a thin atmosphere such as Mars has—Mars has the same surface gravity as Mercury—but orbiting so near the Sun causes the surface of Mercury to be hotter than the inside of an oven (500°F, or 260°C). Whatever gas Mercury might have had moved so fast that it easily escaped the planet's gravity.

If Earth were made only of rock, its gravity would be substantially less than it is. There would be a thinner atmosphere that would not provide nearly as much protection as our existing atmosphere does. In addition to air for breathing, the atmosphere provides pressure, protects the surface from space radiation, moves the Sun's heat around the planet to balance temperatures, and even blocks or burns up most of the meteors that enter Earth's atmosphere from space. Although relatively small in size compared to the whole Earth, the inner and outer core accounts for approximately 33 percent of Earth's total mass. The core contributes greatly to the high gravitational pull that holds a substantial atmosphere around Earth. Without this substantial atmosphere, life, especially human life, would be very different.

LIGHT UP THE NIGHT

You have to live very far north or very far south to see the northern or southern lights. They are also called auroras. In the north, auroras are properly known as aurora borealis and in the south, as aurora australis. Auroras are visible to the eye only on dark nights at very high latitudes. They take on many forms, including the shapes of curtains, veils, rays, and ribbons. Colors range from yellow, green, and red to whitish. The lights dance and swirl across the sky in ghostly images.

Auroras are produced by the interaction of three things—electrically charged radiation from the Sun, thin gas in the upper atmosphere, and magnetism. The light is

Aurora borealis, also called the northern lights, is observed in the night sky, mainly at high latitudes. Aurora borealis occurs when charged and highly energetic particles from the Sun (the solar wind) are drawn by Earth's magnetic field to the northern and southern polar regions. Hundreds of miles (kilometers) up, they collide with the upper atmosphere, causing the excitation of atoms and molecules, which leads to the emission of light.

created when the charged particles strike the atoms of gas. This is similar to what happens inside neon lights used for advertising signs. The bent glass tube of a neon light contains low-pressure neon gas. An electric current travels from neon atom to neon atom inside the tube. As it does, each atom gives off light. The same thing happens to the gas in the upper atmosphere. It glows as it is struck by the charged particles of the Sun. You might wonder why the whole night sky doesn't light up. The charged particles from the Sun usually do not

MAGNETISM AND ELECTRICITY

During the eighteenth and nineteenth centuries, the foundations for understanding Earth's magnetic field were laid. Scientists discovered that magnetism and electricity were directly related. A Danish physicist and teacher by the name of Hans Christian Oersted discovered the relationship. While leading a class, he accidentally brought a magnetic compass near a wire through which an electric current was flowing. The needle deflected from north when it came near the wire. Later, scientists discovered that a moving magnet near a wire could produce an electric current. These discoveries led to the creation of electric generators and electric motors and to the understanding of how currents are produced within the outer core that creates Earth's magnetic field.

Danish physicist Hans Christian Oersted (1777–1851) is shown here with his assistant observing an experiment to demonstrate the effect of an electric current on a magnetic compass needle. This was the first-known demonstration of a connection between electricity and magnetism.

reach Earth's atmosphere in the middle latitudes. That's because of Earth's magnetic field.

Earth has a powerful magnetic field. Sometimes we speak of Earth's magnetism as though a gigantic bar magnet is embedded within Earth. The bar magnet has a north and a south pole, and magnetic compasses point to the north. The magnetic north and south poles are not precisely lined up with the true North and South Poles defined by Earth's axis. Earth spins, or rotates, once around an axis in approximately twenty-four hours. If Earth did have a bar magnet inside, it would be tilted about 11 degrees away from Earth's axis.

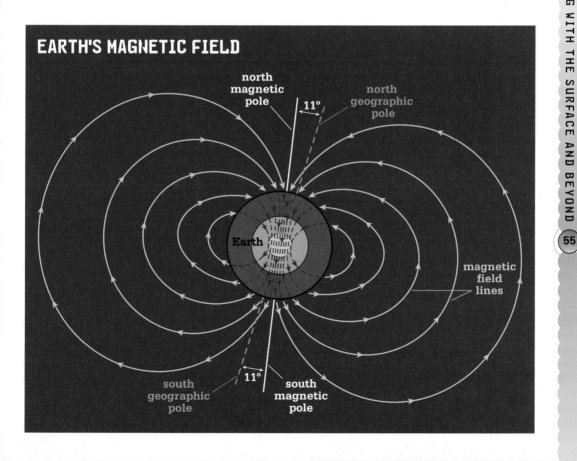

EARTH'S MAGNETIC FIELD

WANDERING POLES

Geologists have a neat trick when they study Earth's magnetic field. When molten rock cools, some of the mineral crystals that form within will have magnetic properties. Like iron filings sprinkled around a magnet, the rock crystals will align themselves with the magnetic force lines of Earth and be frozen in that direction within the rock. They become like permanently aimed compass needles. However, geologists have noticed that magnetic crystals in rocks of different ages point in different directions. This provided key evidence that the continents have been in other orientations and offer clues for reconstructing their positions. The reason for this is that the circulation within the liquid outer core is complicated. Flows gradually shift their directions, and this moves the poles about but only by a few degrees. This can be measured by taking a magnetic compass direction over a period of twenty years or so. The data will show a slight wandering of the poles. By looking at magnetic minerals in rocks of different ages, geologists can plot the path of the continents and the magnetic poles through time.

Geologists have noted that every few hundred thousand to a few million years, Earth's magnetic field reorganizes itself. Realignment in the core circulation causes the north and south magnetic poles to change places. The realignment is sort of like taking a bar magnet, standing it on its end so that north is up and south is down, then turning it upside down. Earth itself doesn't turn over, just its magnetic field.

Pole reversal is of great concern, because of its potential effects on life on Earth. The magnetic field in space protects Earth's surface from dangerous space radiation, and while the poles are flipping, the protection could go away. Geologists are trying to determine when the next reversal will occur.

If you have ever sprinkled iron filings around a bar magnet, you will have observed the iron particles forming lines that loop from the magnet's north to its south pole. If you could do the same with Earth, you would notice the same force lines. The lines start from within Earth at the magnetic poles, pass through the atmosphere, travel way out into space, and then arc back to Earth on the other side. When the charged particles arrive from the Sun, they are captured by Earth's magnetic force lines. The particles spiral around the lines and bounce from the north to the south magnetic poles until they run out of energy. The force lines concentrate the charged particles into a strong stream. As the stream approaches one of the magnetic poles, the magnetic force lines direct the stream down toward the thin upper atmosphere where the gas begins to glow.

Where does Earth's magnetic field come from? The answer is, the core. You might first think that because iron is a magnetic mineral, it is only natural that the iron core is magnetic. Not so. Iron nails can be turned into magnets, but if you heat them, they will lose their magnetism. Although the inner core is solid iron, it is very hot for two reasons. One is that the core still retains some of the heat created when Earth was created billions of years ago, and it is still cooling. The other reason is that the tremendous weight of the crust, mantle, and the core itself heats the core. Just how hot is not certain, but it is estimated to be about as hot as the surface of the Sun, or 11,000°F (6,000°C). That temperature is more than enough to drive away any natural magnetism of the iron.

Earth wouldn't have much of a magnetic field if it weren't for the outer core. Also made mostly of iron, it is liquid. More than just being liquid, the outer core is moving. Geologists have detected weatherlike movement of the materials in the outer core. There appear to be great swirling storm systems similar to the cyclones that occur in Earth's atmosphere.

Where do the movements come from? Geologists have discovered three possible sources for the movement. Most likely, all three work together. First, the inner core is rotating faster than the mantle and crust. Core rotation was discovered by looking at the data from earthquakes. On occasion, a P-wave would arrive a half of a second faster at a seismograph than it should have. The geologists concluded that the immense pressure on the inner core must align the iron crystals. Because of the alignment, earthquake waves would travel slightly faster going with the grain of the crystals than when going across it. You can feel this grain effect by running your hand across some fabrics. Your hand slides easily in one direction, but the other direction feels rougher.

By carefully measuring the differences in P-wave arrivals over many years, geologists concluded that the alignment of the inner core with Earth's surface changes very slowly. The inner core is rotating at its own rate. It is able to do this because the inner core is surrounded by the liquid outer core and not firmly attached to the rest of the planet. The difference in core rotation from surface rotation is slightly less than one degree per year. What that means is that in about 400 years, Earth's inner core will have rotated one more time than Earth's crust. (Several scientists have come up with different measurements for the rate of inner core rotation. Some have estimated the complete extra rotation of the core to take only 120 years. Regardless of the different estimates, scientists do agree that the inner core rotates slightly faster than the entire planet.)

Earth's core spins about 0.3 to 0.5 degrees faster than Earth every year. That may not seem like much, but it is about fifty thousand times faster than the plates carrying the continents move across Earth's surface.

Since the inner core is moving at a different rate than the rest of the planet, friction produces movements within the liquid outer core. Another source for movement in the outer core are heat currents. Watch a pot of soup on a stove as it heats up. Currents begin appearing. Soup at the top of the pot spreads out from several points as hot soup wells up from the bottom. The cooler soup at the top falls to the bottom, where it is heated, and then rises back to the surface. The upwelling and falling of the soup in the pot is driven by what are called convection currents. Similar currents exist within the molten outer core.

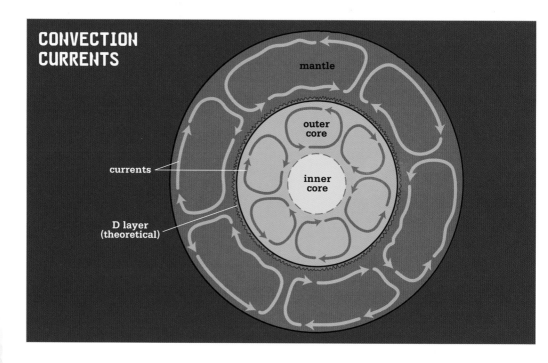

CONVECTION CURRENTS

mantle

outer core

inner core

currents

D layer (theoretical)

The tremendous heat stored in the inner core is gradually being released through Earth's surface. It is a terribly slow process. Once, long ago, the entire Earth was molten. As cooling took place, the surface hardened. So did the inner core and the lower mantle. In billions of years, Earth will cool off enough to solidify as Mars has. In the meantime, the convection currents within the outer core cause great upwellings of superheated molten rock to rise and cool but still-hot molten rock to sink.

In Earth's atmosphere, upwelling and sinking of the atmosphere combined with its movement across the surface creates great whirlpools of air masses, called cyclones. Looking for similar effects within Earth, scientists have discovered a great whirlpool within the upper core that circles around the northern end of Earth's axis. They predict that a similar whirlpool will be found circling the southern end of the axis but haven't found it yet because there isn't enough data from there to reach any conclusions.

A third source of movement is believed to be the boundary between the outer core and the lower mantle. The boundary is actually a narrow irregular zone, called the D layer. It is only 130 to 200 miles (200 to 300 km) thick. In this zone, iron crystallizes on the lower surface of the mantle. Other elements in the outer core, such as oxygen, sulfur, and silicon, rise to the D layer where the temperatures are 1,800°F (1,000°C) cooler. These elements begin forming a slushy mass of mineral crystals as the elements combine. As the crystals form, they become denser than the liquid that they cooled from. Occasionally, large masses of the crystals break off and fall back into the outer core. As the crystals fall, heat up, and melt, they create vertical currents that drag material from below to fill up the gap where the crystals fell from. The effect on the liquid outer core is the same as the effect of heat-driven convection currents. If this process is actually

Convection within Earth's mantle moves the semisolid rock at an average rate of about 1.6 inches (4 centimeters) per year. Since the formation of Earth more than 4 billion years ago, materials in the mantle of Earth have moved about 60,000 miles (97,000 km).

happening, it should produce great swirls in the molten rock. Inner core rotation, convection currents, and possibly avalanches of crystal masses drive the movements of the outer core. Scientists believe that the moving outer core is the source of Earth's magnetic field. The movements create a dynamo. A dynamo is a machine that generates electricity. It is made of a magnet at the end of a shaft. The magnet is made to rotate within a coil of wire. The magnetic field of the magnet moves as the magnet spins, and this generates an electric current in the wire. Because Earth acts like a dynamo, it is called a geodynamo.

SPINNING THE CORE

The very slow but widespread movements within the molten outer core of Earth generate a powerful electric current. This current, in turn, produces a planetwide magnetic field, and the magnetic field creates more electric current. The effect accumulates to an estimated billion-ampere current that moves across the boundary between the outer and inner core. This current and its magnetic effects combine to exert forces on the inner core, rotating it slowly like an electric motor. In addition, Earth's rotation is slowing down, due to the friction from tides caused by the gravitational pull of the Moon. The tides drag on the crust and the mantle and make them rotate more slowly than the core.

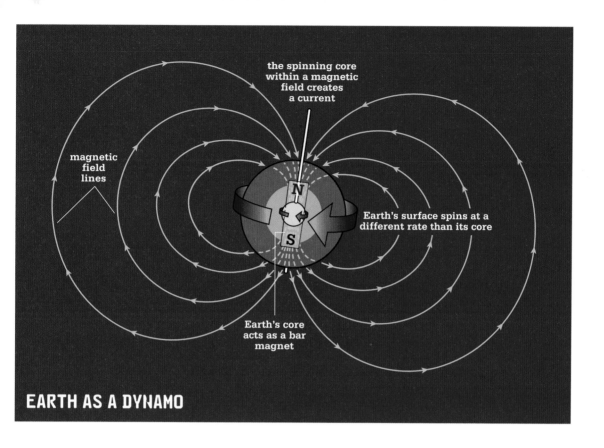

the spinning core
within a magnetic
field creates
a current

magnetic
field
lines

Earth's surface spins at a
different rate than its core

Earth's core
acts as a bar
magnet

EARTH AS A DYNAMO

Inside the outer core, swirls of molten iron sweep past one another. Each atom of iron has its own very tiny magnetic field. Because the iron is molten, atoms point in all directions, so there is not a dominant magnetic-field direction of the kind that can be created in solid iron. However, as the atoms sweep past one another, the little magnetic fields of the individual atoms induce electric currents in one another. The currents create more magnetism, which induces more currents, which creates more magnetism, and so on. As a result, a powerful magnetic field is created inside Earth that extends out into space, captures charged particles from the Sun, and makes auroras possible, as shown in the diagram on the following page.

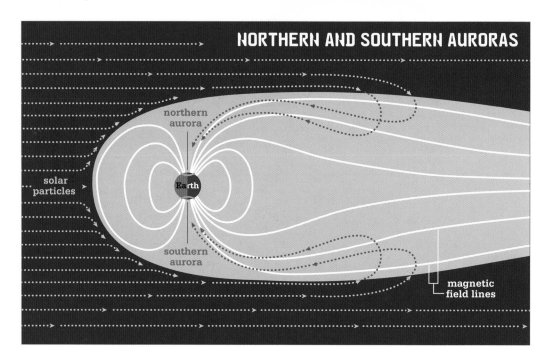

northern aurora

solar particles

Earth

southern aurora

magnetic field lines

MOVEMENTS OF EARTH'S CRUST

Earth's surface is a wonderland of mountains, valleys, gorges, plains, and huge ocean basins. Forces both inside and out of it are constantly shaping the surface. The inside forces thrust up land and move the continents about. The outside forces (running water, wind, and ice) wear away and erode the land surface. Gravity from inside the planet propels rivers that take the sediment produced by weathering and deposits it in the ocean basins.

Without the internal forces from Earth's mantle and below, erosion at the surface would eventually wear away all land surfaces and deposit them in the ocean basins. Earth would have a planetwide ocean whose surface would be broken only by large ice sheets produced at the poles. Fortunately, the internal and external forces are balanced, and therefore, Earth has continents and islands dotting the ocean's surface.

Two things contribute to the creation of new land on the surface. Both depend on Earth's elastic mantle. As mountains are slowly worn down and deposited in ocean basins, heavy, thick layers of sediment pile up in ocean basins near the shore. Gradually, pressure builds up, and the sediment changes into rock. The weight of the rock is tremendous, and it presses the crust into the mantle. Over millions of years, the slow-moving plates in Earth's crust heat and compress the new rock and add it to the edges of the continents. At the same time, the collisions of the plates thrust the new rock upward to form new landmasses above the ocean. Once exposed on the surface, water and wind and other forces erode the rock at the top away. With less

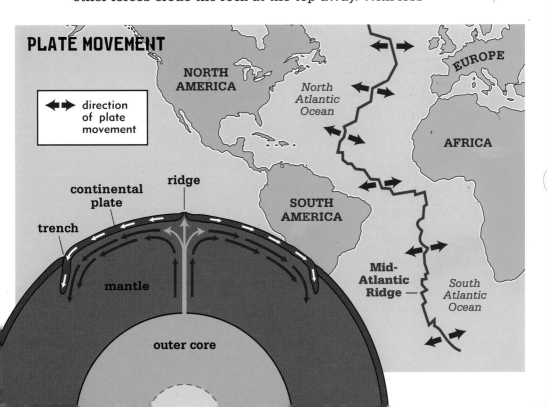

PLATE MOVEMENT

◀▶ direction of plate movement

NORTH AMERICA

North Atlantic Ocean

EUROPE

AFRICA

continental plate

ridge

trench

SOUTH AMERICA

mantle

Mid-Atlantic Ridge —

South Atlantic Ocean

outer core

weight pressing it down, the mantle rebounds and lifts lower rocks to higher elevations.

The other effect of the mantle has to do with its convection currents. Upwelling hot zones in the mantle put pressure on the crustal rock above. The rock splits, and hot lava reaches the surface of the crust. One great zone of upward pressure is a zigzagging chain of mountains beneath the North and South Atlantic oceans. The chain is splitting apart, and new volcanic rock is forming in the crack. The force is tremendous, and it moves the ocean crust on either side of the chain outward. This, in turn, pushes North and South America westward and Europe, Africa, and Asia eastward.

The leading edges of the crust carrying the continents slides over the thinner, denser ocean crust. As the ocean crust subducts, or moves under, some of the rock is melted and forms great blobs of magma. The magma rises toward the surface, creating earthquakes and eventually volcanoes. If the magma does not reach the surface, it cools into granitic rocks and forms a mountain. Look at a world map, and you will see that most of the great mountain chains of the world ring the Pacific Ocean basin. Not only is the ring laced with mountains, but it is also the place where the greatest number of active volcanoes is found and most earthquakes occur. The pressure of the rising magma cracks the land and, when earthquakes occur, the land shifts. The cracks also open pathways for molten rock from the mantle to reach the surface and erupt as lava.

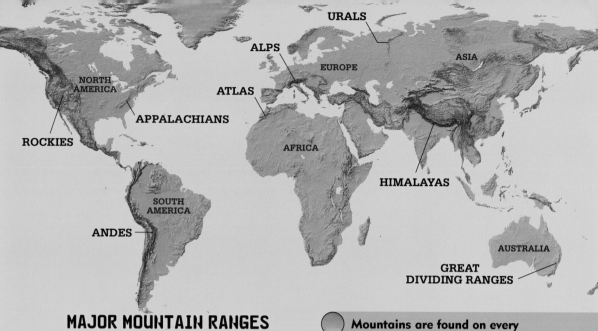

URALS

ALPS

EUROPE

ASIA

NORTH
AMERICA

ATLAS

APPALACHIANS

ROCKIES

AFRICA

SOUTH
AMERICA

HIMALAYAS

ANDES

AUSTRALIA

GREAT
DIVIDING RANGES

MAJOR MOUNTAIN RANGES

Mountains are found on every continent and many islands of the world. Thrust upward by the same forces that move the world's tectonic plates, mountains form long chains and ranges such as the Rockies, Appalachians, Himalayas, and Alps. Mixed in with the tectonic mountains are volcanic mountains built from repeated lava eruptions.

In these ways, the land is rebuilt. Convection currents in the mantle drive land-building processes on the surface. Fortunately, the currents move very slowly, only about 1.6 inches (4 cm) per year. In turn, the crust moves very slowly. The crust under most of North America moves at about the same rate as your fingernails grow. If the rate were much faster, the ring around the Pacific Ocean would be far more violent than it is today. It would not be a good place to live. Considering the very slow rate of mantle convection, one might wonder how the mountains around the Pacific Ocean got so large. The answer is very simple—time. We naturally think in terms of our life spans. In the life span of Earth, we are but a moment. When there are hundreds of millions of years to work with, tall mountains are easy.

MISSION TO THE CORE

In science fiction, a trip to Earth's core is not only possible, it also makes a good story. In *A Journey to the Center of the Earth*, Jules Verne had his heroes descend to the center of Earth by following an interconnecting maze of volcanic tunnels. Edgar Rice Burroughs, in his book *At the Earth's Core*, had his heroes make the trip in a mechanical subterranean prospector vehicle. In *The Core*, a 2003 movie, a subterranean ship called the *Virgil* carried heroes to the center so that they could restart the core spinning after it had been stopped by a secret weapons project. Unfortunately, there aren't any deep volcanic caves, and no subterranean prospector vehicles have yet been built. Trips to Earth's core are still the stuff of science fiction—at least so far.

JULES VERNE'S **JOURNEY** TO THE **CENTER** OF THE **EARTH**

1001 WONDERS!
The Lost City of Atlantis!
The Prehistoric Dimetrodons!
The Crater of Snakells-Jökull!
The Subterranean Oceans!

1001 THRILLS!
The Giant Mushroom Forest!
The Stratum of Cinnabar!
Gargantuan Chameleons with 20 feet tongues!
Stalagmites and Stalactites!

STARRING

PAT BOONE · JAMES MASON
ARLENE DAHL · DIANE BAKER COLOR by DE LUXE
CINEMASCOPE

PRODUCED BY   DIRECTED BY   SCREENPLAY BY
CHARLES BRACKETT · HENRY LEVIN · WALTER REISCH and **CHARLES BRACKETT**   20 Century-Fox

The movie version of Jules Verne's *Journey to the Center of the Earth* boasts "1001 WONDERS! 1001 THRILLS!" but in reality, such a theoretically possible journey would feature 1,001 technical challenges!

A real trip to the core is very unlikely but not necessarily impossible. Scientist David J. Stevenson, of the California Institute of Technology, has a plan that could work. Stevenson envisions a grapefruit-sized robotic probe that would be sent to Earth's core. The probe would have various scientific instruments that would measure temperature, chemical composition, and electrical properties of the core. The information it collected would be sent back to the surface using low-frequency sound waves that would be received by special detectors.

Stevenson's trip to the core wouldn't involve drilling. The deepest drill holes only go down about 7 miles (12 km). That is about one-three-hundredth of the distance the probe would have to travel to reach the core's boundary. Instead, Stevenson proposes sending the probe through cracks reaching 2,000 miles (3,000 km) into Earth. However, there is a problem. No crack goes anywhere near that deep. If a crack were to open in just the asthenosphere, it would soon close, because the

PIECE OF THE CORE?

From rocks collected in northern California, southwestern Oregon, Hawaii, and Siberia, some geologists believe they have material that may have originated in Earth's core. Stationary hot spots in the mantle such as the one that is building the Hawaiian Islands may originate much deeper inside Earth than once thought. Many scientists believe hot spots begin just 60 miles (100 km) below the crust. However, the new rock samples offer clues that hot spots may go much deeper, perhaps 1,700 miles (2,700 km). The rocks have small crystals that contain large amounts of the element osmium. Osmium is rare in the crust. It is found in iron meteorites and is believed to be plentiful in Earth's core. Geologists studying the rocks believe the crystals began forming near the boundary of the core and mantle and so will provide information about what that part of Earth is like.

asthenosphere is elastic and the slowly flowing rock would shut it. Stevenson's idea, which sounds fantastic, is to make his own crack.

Stevenson proposes to create a wide crack by blasting Earth's surface with explosives. The explosives would consist of a few thousand tons (metric tons) of TNT or, more conveniently, a nuclear bomb. It would have to create the force of a moderate earthquake but focused in a small area of the crust. By itself, the explosion would not open a crack all the way to the core. The explosion would just get the crack started. Immediately after the explosion, the crack would be filled with several hundred thousand to several million tons (metric tons) of molten iron. The mass and heat of the molten iron would force the crack to spread beneath it. No wider than about 12 inches (30 cm) in any one place, the crack would permit the iron to travel farther downward where it would force the crack to continue to spread. According to Stevenson, this would all take place at roughly the speed a person could run. The small size of the probe would permit it to slide through the crack along with the molten iron. In a week, the probe would arrive at the core, where it would do its work. Most likely, the mission to the core would consist of several probes, in case one got stuck on the way down or just stopped working.

Stevenson estimates that the cost of the mission would be about $10 billion—considerably less than the cost of the space missions we have sent to the other

HOLLOW EARTH

The idea of a hollow Earth was first proposed in 1692 by English astronomer Edmund Halley (of Halley's comet fame). Halley believed Earth consisted of three concentric spheres surrounding a small core in its center. In the eighteenth century, Leonhard Euler of Switzerland replaced Halley's multiple spheres with a single open space in which a small Sun was located. Euler suggested Earth's crust had large holes at the North and South Poles and it would be possible to travel through them into Earth's interior. American John Cleves Symmes Jr., in the early nineteenth century, tried to organize expeditions to the poles to find these holes and people living inside Earth. While these ideas seem silly in light of our understanding of Earth's interior, hollow Earth stories have not gone away. There are still fringe groups that believe in a hollow Earth, and proposals for expeditions to find the entrances are still being made.

planets. The things we might find on the way to the core could be just as exciting as the discoveries made on other worlds.

It is highly unlikely that traveling to Earth's core along a forced crack will ever happen, and most scientists think the plan wouldn't work. Furthermore, worldwide public opinion would probably not look kindly at any plans for penetrating the planet. However, proposals like this one inspire others to come up with different ideas. Someday, a practical approach to traveling within the Earth may be found.

For now, we have to be content with seismographs, magnetometers, thermometers, rock and mineral samples from volcanoes and ancient mountains, and meteorites from space. In spite of not being able to travel within the Earth or even send robotic probes there, much has been learned about Earth's inside. We know its layers and its general composition. We know its temperature. We know how it moves and how it generates magnetic fields. We are just beginning to understand all the different ways in which Earth's core and mantle affect Earth's surface, water, and air, and how they help to shape our lives.

Scientists are piecing together the jigsaw puzzle that is Earth.

The Japanese ship *Chikyu* hopes to drill 4.4 miles (7 km) through Earth's crust and into its mantle. If its attempt, starting in 2007, is successful, it will more than triple the record for drilling through oceanic crust and bring up samples of the mantle for study.

GLOSSARY

accretion disk: a stage in the evolution of the solar system when the nebula began to swirl and flatten out into a disk shape

asteroid: a large space rock tens of yards (m) to hundreds of miles (km) across that formed from the materials in the solar system nebula

asthenosphere: the upper elastic portion of the mantle, upon which the crust moves

atmosphere: the shell of air that surrounds Earth

aurora: light given off by upper atmosphere gases when they are struck by charged particles ejected by the Sun

biosphere: the thin layer of the surface of Earth where life exists

comet: a large mass of ice, rock, and dust that formed from the materials in the solar system nebula

core: the iron sphere that is found in Earth's center

crust: the rocky surface layer of Earth

density: a measure of the amount of matter contained in something compared to the matter in an equal volume of water

dynamo: an electric generator consisting of a rotating magnet inside a coil of wire

echolocation: using reflected sound waves to determine the direction and distance to objects

exosphere: the uppermost layer of Earth's atmosphere extending out to 6,000 miles (10,000 km) from Earth's surface

geodynamo: the dynamo effect created by the movement of molten iron in Earth's outer core

gravity: a force that causes all matter to be attracted to all other matter

hydrosphere: the shell of water found on or near Earth's surface in oceans, rivers, groundwater, ice, and the atmosphere

light-year: the distance light travels in one year's time in a vacuum (5.8 trillion miles/9.3 trillion km)

lithosphere: Earth's crust and the upper level of the mantle

L-wave: a surface earthquake wave that rolls up and down

magma: molten rock beneath Earth's surface

magnetic field: the area around Earth or a magnet where the magnetic force can be felt

mantle: the thick layer of rock beneath Earth's crust

mass: how much matter is contained in an object (usually measured in kilograms)

meteor: a bit of space metal or rock that formed from the leftover materials in the solar system nebula

meteorite: a piece of space rock or metal that falls to Earth's surface

nebula: a great cloud of gas and dust out of which our solar system formed

nuclear fusion: the process by which the Sun converts hydrogen into helium and releases light and heat into space

P-wave: a primary or push-pull earthquake wave

seismograph: a recording device that measures the occurrence, duration, and strength of earthquakes

seismoscope: a device that indicates when an earthquake has occurred

supernova: a gigantic explosion of a star that creates a bright flare hundreds of millions of times more brilliant than the star and leaves behind an expanding gas cloud

S-wave: a secondary or shearing earthquake wave

BIBLIOGRAPHY

Ahern, J. L. "Seismology and Earth's Interior." *Judson L. Ahern*. 2004. http://geophysics.ou.edu/solid_earth/notes/seismology/seismo_interior/seismo_interior.html (June 21, 2006).

Alden, Andrew. "About Earth's Core." *About.com*. N.d. http://geology.about.com/od/core/a/about_the_core.htm (June 21, 2006).

Bobick, J. E., ed. *The Handy Science Answer Book*. Centennial edition. Pittsburgh: Carnegie Library of Pittsburgh, 2005.

Geology/Geophysics 101. "Earth's Interior." *Honolulu Community College*. August 27, 2004. http://honolulu.hawaii.edu/distance/gg101/Programs/program4%20EarthInterior/program4.html (June 21, 2006).

Hamblin, W. K., and E. H. Christiansen. *Earth's Dynamic Systems*. Englewood Cliffs, NJ: Prentice-Hall, Inc., 1996.

Lambert, David. *The Field Guide to Geology*. New York: Checkmark Books, 1997.

Luhr, J. F., ed. *Smithsonian Earth*. London: Dorling Kindersley, 2003.

Mathez, E. A., ed. *Earth Inside and Out*. American Museum of Natural History series. New York: W. W. Norton & Company, 2001.

Mathez, E. A., and J. D. Webster. *The Earth Machine*. New York: Columbia University Press, 2004.

Smith, G., and A. Pun. *How Does Earth Work: Physical Geology and the Process of Science*. Upper Saddle River, NJ: Prentice Hall, 2006.

FOR FURTHER INFORMATION

Books

DK E. Guides. *Explore Earth*. New York: Dorling Kindersley, 2004.

Downs, Sandra. *Earth's Fiery Fury*. Minneapolis: Twenty-First Century Books, 2000.

Gallant, Roy. *Exploring Earth's Interior*. New York: Benchmark Investigative Group, 2002.

Harris, Nicholas. *Journey to the Center of the Earth*. Pleasantville, NY: Reader's Digest, 1999.

Johnson, Rebecca L. *Plate Tectonics*. Minneapolis: Twenty-First Century Books, 2006.

Lafleur, Claude. *Inside the Earth*. Milwaukee: World Almanac, 2001.

Lindop, Laurie. *Probing Volcanoes*. Minneapolis: Twenty-First Century Books, 2003.

Miller, Ron. *Earth and the Moon*. Minneapolis: Twenty-First Century Books, 2003.

Scholastic Atlas of Earth. New York: Scholastic Reference, 2005.

Silverstein, Alvin, Virginia Silverstein, and Laura Silverstein Nunn. *Plate Tectonics*. Minneapolis: Twenty-First Century Books, 1998.

Websites

Braile, Larry, and Sheryl Braile. "3-D Earth Structure Model." *L Braile Home Page.* September 2005. http://www.eas.purdue.edu/~braile/edumod/threedearth/threedearth.htm
This website offers instructions for constructing a 3-D model of Earth's interior.

Hamilton, Rosanna L. "Earth's Interior and Plate Tectonics." *Views of the Solar System.* 1997. http://www.solarviews.com/eng/earthint.htm
A multimedia adventure unfolds the splendor of the Sun, planets, moons, comets, astroids, and more.

Smithsonian National Museum of Natural History. "Inside Earth." *The Dynamic Earth.* N.d. http://www.mnh.si.edu/earth/text/3_2_1_0.html
Visitors to this site will find a discussion of how plate tectonics and volcanoes change Earth's surface. Links take viewers to pages with information on Earth's history as seen through its stones.

Southern California Integrated GPS Network. "Structure of the Earth. *SCIGN Education Module.* August 14, 1998. http://scign.jpl.nasa.gov/learn/plate1.htm
This website has information on the structure of Earth. It includes interactive diagrams and some excellent links to material on plate tectonics.

ThinkQuest. "Earth's Structure." *Spaceship Earth*. 2002.
http://mediatheek.thinkquest.nl/~ll125/en/struct.htm
Find information and diagrams about Earth's core, mantle, and
crust.

U.S. Geological Survey. "Inside the Earth." *This Dynamic Earth:
The Story of Plate Techtonics*. January 29, 2001. http://pubs
.usgs.gov/publications/text/inside.html
Viewers will find a cutaway diagram showing the internal
structures of Earth.

INDEX

ABOUT THE AUTHOR

Gregory L. Vogt holds a doctor of education degree in curriculum and instruction from Oklahoma State University. He began his professional career as a science teacher. He later joined NASA's education programs teaching students and teachers about space exploration. He works in outreach programs for the Kennedy Space Center. He also serves as an educational consultant to Delaware North Parks Services of Spaceport and is the principal investigator for an educational grant with the National Space Biomedical Research Institute. Vogt has written more than seventy children's science trade books.

PHOTO ACKNOWLEDGMENTS

The images in this book are used with the permission of: PhotoDisc Royalty Free by Getty Images, (lava: main and center ring), (cracked earth: second ring), (vegetation: fourth ring), (sky/clouds: fifth ring), all backgrounds, pp. 2–3, 6, 8, 18, 25, 29, 32, 37, 41, 42, 47, 50, 59, 61, 68, 73; MedioImages Royalty Free by Getty Images, (water: third ring), all backgrounds, p. 2; NASA (stars/nebula: sixth ring), (earth), all backgrounds, pp. 2–3, 9; © Laura Westlund/Independent Picture Service, pp. 10, 12, 14, 15, 19, 21, 24, 26, 27, 28, 40, 44, 55, 60, 63, 64, 65, 67; © Kevin Fleming/CORBIS, p. 11; © David A. Hardy/Photo Researchers, Inc., p. 13; © Jim Sugar/CORBIS, p. 17; © Science Museum/Science & Society Picture Library, p. 22; © Reuters/CORBIS, p. 23; AP/Wide World Photos, p. 31; © NASA/Science Source/Photo Researchers, Inc., p. 33; © Roger Ressmeyer/CORBIS, p. 34; Courtesy of Dr. Søren Gregersen, Seismic Division KMS, Denmark, p. 36; © Marli Miller/Visuals Unlimited, p. 38; U.S. Geological Survey/Photo by D.A. Swanson, p. 46 (top); National Park Service Photo by George Marler, p. 46 (bottom); © johnbetts – fineminerals.com, p. 48; © Bryan R. White – www .astro-photo.com, p. 53; The Granger Collection, New York, p. 54; © Photo by 20th Century Fox/Hulton Archive/Courtesy of Getty Images, p. 69. Front Cover: PhotoDisc Royalty Free by Getty Images, (lava: main and center ring), (cracked earth: second ring), (vegetation: fourth ring), (sky/clouds: fifth ring); MedioImages Royalty Free by Getty Images, (water: third ring); NASA, (stars/nebula: sixth ring). Back Cover: PhotoDisc Royalty Free by Getty Images, (lava); NASA, (earth). Spine: PhotoDisc Royalty Free by Getty Images, (lava).